About This Book

Title: *Shells*

Step: 3

Word Count: 115

Skills in Focus: Digraph sh

Tricky Words: sea, beach, their, live, water, new, halves, too, empty

Ideas For Using This Book

Before Reading:

- **Comprehension:** Look at the title and cover image together. Ask readers what they know about shells. What new things do they think they might learn in this book?
- **Accuracy:** Practice saying the tricky words listed on page 1.
- **Phonics and Phonemic Awareness:** Have readers look at the book's title. Help them blend the sounds they see in the word *shells*. Bring attention to the *sh* in the word. Explain that this is a digraph, two letters that make one sound when they are together. Ask readers to say *shells* again and help them tap their finger for each sound in the word. Emphasize the /sh/ and say it louder as you tap. Do the tapping again but say the /sh/ quieter this time to emphasize it. Ask readers to watch for other *sh* digraphs in the text.

During Reading:

- Have readers point under each word as they read it.
- **Decoding:** If readers are stuck on a word, help them say each sound and blend the sounds together smoothly. Be sure to point out any *sh* digraph sounds.
- **Comprehension:** Invite students to talk about what new things they are learning about shells while reading. What are they learning that they didn't know before?

After Reading:

Discuss the book. Some ideas for questions:

- Have you ever found a seashell at the beach? What did it look like?
- What different types of shells have you seen before?

Shells

Text by Laura Stickney

Reading Consultant
Deborah MacPhee, PhD
Professor, School of Teaching and Learning
Illinois State University

PICTURE WINDOW BOOKS
a capstone imprint

Lots of shells
slosh in the sea.

Shells sit on sand
at the beach.

Things live in shells.
A snail has a shell.

Crabs live in shells.

Then crabs shed their shells.

Crabs shed shells in sand.

Then crabs
get new shells.

The sea can push shells.
It pulls shells too.

Shells shift in the sea.
Fish swim past shells.

Conch shells have twists and bumps.

Conch shells have prongs, shafts, and crests.

Shells can be
as flat as fans.

A clam shell has two halves.
The shell can shut.

Shells can crack.
Shells can chip.
Do not smash thin shells!

Pick up empty shells.
Brush sand off shells.
Swish and splash
shells in water.

More Ideas:

Phonemic Awareness Activity

Practicing Digraph *sh*:

Say the story words *shell*, *shed*, and *shut*. Have readers tap out the sounds down their arm, once for each sound, starting by their shoulders. Ask readers how many sounds they hear in the word. Continue with words that have more than three sounds, such as *splash*, *brush*, *slosh*, and *shift*.

Extended Learning Activity

Seashell Story:

Ask readers to draw a seashell on a piece of paper. Ask readers to imagine what type of animal might live in the shell. Then ask readers to write three sentences about the animal and its shell. Have students use /sh/ sounds in their sentences.

Published by Picture Window Books, an imprint of Capstone
1710 Roe Crest Drive, North Mankato, Minnesota 56003
capstonepub.com

Library of Congress Cataloging-in-Publication Data is available on the Library of Congress website.

ISBN: 9798875227059 (hardback)
ISBN: 9798875229947 (paperback)
ISBN: 9798875229923 (eBook PDF)

Image Credits: iStock: Arnaud Abadie, 14–15, fcafotodigital, cover, johndmartin, 2–3, zoranm, 12–13; Shutterstock: Alexey Masliy, 19, Damir Zurub, 4, Ethan Daniels, 17, 24, Irene Castro, 5, Kate La Carte, 6–7, Mega Pixel, 1, 16, nukopic, 10–11, patpitchaya, 22–23, qingqing, 8, Rapax, 9, Ray Geiger, 20–21, StacieStauffSmith Photos, 18

Printed and bound in China. 6274